PRAIRIE
DREAMS

PRAIRIE
DREAMS

COURTNEY MILNE

WESTERN PRODUCER PRAIRIE BOOKS
Saskatoon, Saskatchewan

Cover photographs by Courtney Milne
Cover and book design by McKay Goettler and Associates
Colour separations by True Color Graphics Limited

Printed and bound in Canada
10 9 8 7 6 5 4 3 2 1

The publisher acknowledges the support received for this publication from the Canada Council.

Western Producer Prairie Books is a unique publishing venture located in the middle of western Canada and owned by a group of prairie farmers who are members of Saskatchewan Wheat Pool. From the first book in 1954, a reprint of a serial originally carried in the weekly newspaper *The Western Producer*, to the book before you now, the tradition of providing enjoyable and informative reading for all Canadians is continued.

Canadian Cataloguing in Publication Data

Milne, Courtney, 1943–

    Prairie dreams

    ISBN: 0-88833-295-5

1. Photography – Prairie Provinces – Landscapes.
2. Prairie Provinces – Description and travel –
1981– – Views*.   3. Milne, Courtney, 1943–.
I. Title.

FC3234.2.M556 1989   779′.9971203   C89-098064-0
F1060.M556 1989

Extracts from the following works have been reprinted with permission:

Between the Red and the Rockies by Grant MacEwan, with permission from Western Producer Prairie Books
The Gates of the Sun by Sharon Butala, with permission from Fifth House
In the Blue Night Soup I Can Hear the Night Hawk Whistle by Graeme Card, with permission from Graeme Card
The Last Spike by Pierre Berton, with permission from Pierre Berton Enterprises
Letters by Nancy Russell, with permission from the Saskatoon *Star Phoenix*
My Heart Soars by Chief Dan George, with permission from Hancock House Publishers Limited
A New Improved Sky, "Watercolours of the Prairie" by Don Kerr, with permission from Don Kerr
The Selena Tree by Patricia Joudry, with permission from the Canadian Publishers, McClelland and Stewart, Toronto
Who Has Seen the Wind by W. O. Mitchell, with permission from Macmillan of Canada, a Division of Canada Publishing
    Corporation
Why Shoot the Teacher by Max Braithwaite, with permission from the Canadian Publishers, McClelland and Stewart, Toronto
Wolf Willow by Wallace Stegner, with permission from Macmillan of Canada, a Division of Canada Publishing Corporation

Credits appearing with each extract are hereby made part of this copyright page.

The author has made every effort to obtain permission to reprint material still in copyright. The publisher would be pleased to hear from anyone who has details about uncredited material and will make corrections to subsequent editions of this book.

CONTENTS

For my nephews, Leif and Karl, two intrepid young adventurers with prairie in their blood, and for Heidi Miller, whose poem, "I am the Old One," inspired me to make *Prairie Dreams* come true.

PREFACE AND ACKNOWLEDGEMENTS

On December 3, 1985, I performed my multimedia show, "Prairie Light," for a highly spirited audience in Lloydminster, Alberta. After the performance, a petite ten-year-old girl named Heidi Miller approached me and in a tiny voice asked if she could read me a poem she had written about what the prairie meant to her. While packing my equipment, my hands were stilled as I heard this child speak with the wisdom of an Indian chief. If she can produce a piece of writing that gripping, I pondered, I wonder what other prairie people might write about their involvement with the land.

At that moment, the seed for *Prairie Dreams* was planted. I could not let the idea rest. The following spring I spread the word through a hundred newspapers, asking people to write to me about what the prairie meant to them. Denny Carr of CFQC radio in Saskatoon, and Peter Gzowski on CBC's "Morningside," broadcast the message across Canada, and several television shows gave me a platform.

Like so many prairie harvests, my return was plentiful. In fact, it was a bumper crop. I received over one thousand pieces of prose and poetry from more than two hundred writers. The resulting swath cut across all three Prairie Provinces, all age groups, and every walk of life. The task of sorting wheat from chaff proved more difficult than I had anticipated, however, and refining the product took many months of labour. I hired a full-time editor, Louise Kozroski, and we chose two hundred writings and four hundred photographs as a starting point, then began to search for themes that would lay the groundwork for the chapters of the book. Three years later, *Prairie Dreams* has seen countless revisions, but the initial intent has remained: to produce a book of photographs and writings that reflect the dreams of all prairie people.

I wish firstly to thank all of you who made the effort to write. Thank you as well to the newspaper editors and the radio and television news people who so willingly helped to get the message out. Thank you, Louise, for your monumental help in compiling the work. Thanks also to Nora Russell for the exacting and demanding job of fine tuning, and to Cheryl Sacks and Adele Curtis who looked at the project from a photography-as-art perspective. A special thanks to Lois Nickel for holding the fort for three years while I was out shooting more pictures, and to Sherrill Miller for her helpful guidance and loving support.

Thanks are also due to Gordon McKay for his work with the jacket and book design, and to Jack and Johnny Sutherland for the superb job on the colour separations.

But like the team of oxen that drove our forefather's plough, we have done enough for one season. Let's unhitch the harness of our labours, take a stroll around the old homestead, and begin with a little dreaming backwards.

DREAMING BACKWARDS

The history of the Great Plains is relatively young. Barely a hundred years have passed since the railway pushed through to the West and unloaded its first settlers. In 1883 a group led by John Lake arrived to found a temperance colony on the banks of the Saskatchewan. Their dream was to escape the religious persecution that had forced them to leave their homelands, to start anew, to find their Shangri-la in the land of milk and honey. Though there were more mosquitoes than honey bees, and more coyotes than cows, it was a beginning. They called their new home Saskatoon, after the Indian name for the wild berry that grew in abundance around the settlement.

These pioneers, however, were not the first white men to see the prairie. In 1684, two hundred years earlier, Henry Kelsey, a mere lad in his teens, arrived at York Factory on Hudson Bay to expand the fur trade in the name of England. Six years later, travelling west and south, he eventually reached the Touchwood Hills, near the centre of the Great Plains. Another 120 years of

nomadic Indian life would pass before Lewis and Clark approached the plains from Montana. They were the first to glimpse its southernmost reaches.

There are many places on the Saskatchewan River where I enjoy dreaming of the past, picturing the land and the river as though for the first time. As I watch and photograph, the current swirls in an endless trail of eddies, sleeplessly, as timeless as a dream.

At night I lie tucked into a sleeping bag, the roof over my head a dome of midnight black etched with the effervescent shimmer of the northern lights and studded with the brilliance of a million stars. That experience, too, is timeless, moving me beyond the confines of place and time, back into the prehistory of the Great Plains.

At dawn, as I sit overlooking an uninhabited ravine and absorbing the dry earthiness of dying grasses, I not only hear the pounding of a thousand buffalo hoofs, but also feel their spirits in the restless cry of the wind. And my attempts to record in photographs the untouched, untamed corners of land and sky make me ever aware of the fleetingness of our present-day existence.

Dreaming backwards gives us perspective. It puts our lives in context and makes us aware of our heritage. A visit to a weathered homestead that refuses to bow to the winds is a tangible link with the past, and perhaps by returning to these sites we can rekindle something of the pioneer spirit in ourselves, a vision of their hopes and dreams igniting new passions by reaffirming old values.

"Dreaming Backwards" is a walk through history, a chance to reflect and relive some of those early days.

In May, 1805, the six canoes and two pirogues of the Lewis and Clark expedition were working up the Missouri between the mouth of the Yellowstone and the Musselshell. . . .

They came watchfully, for they were the first. They came stiffened with resolution and alert with wonder. . . .

May 8 brought them to the mouth of a large river emptying into the Missouri from the northwest. It looked to be navigable for boats and pirogues, and for canoes perhaps a long way, for it carried a strong flow of milky-white water and seemed to drain a great reach of country to the north. They looked up it with the eye of imagination: like the White Earth and other northern tributaries they had passed, this one intrigued them as a possible way to the Saskatchewan and the fur country of Prince Rupert's Land, bitterly contested by the Hudson's Bay Company and the Northwesters. . . .

WALLACE STEGNER, FROM WOLF WILLOW, PP. 39-40

Out here, far more than in the brushy Missouri bottoms, the explorers would have found a land with no transition between earth and sky: in the heat the horizons melted and ran; on the flats the sky and clouds moved in the reflecting sloughs. . . .

They did not go north, and did not see it. In 1805 nobody had been as close as they, and their brief speculative stare at the southern edge of the region was the last look any white man would give it for more than a half century.

WALLACE STEGNER, FROM WOLF WILLOW, PP. 41-42

first feet print the sand
  poles test the depth
    gauge the current
hearts beat faster
  at the point of each new bend
anticipate the telling of it after

outrageous plans take shape
and victories that may never be
       loom large

but what else can you do
in a land whose history
you do not know?

LOUISE KOZROSKI, "ON THE RIVERBANK 1884"

Onward the track moved, cutting the plains in two. . . . As it travelled westward it pushed through a country of memories and old bones—furrowed trails fashioned decades before by thousands of bison moving in single file towards the water, vast fields of grey and withered herbage, dead lakes rimmed with tell-tale crusts of alkali. Day by day it crept towards the horizon where, against the gold of the sunset, flocks of fluttering wildfowl, disturbed by the clamour of the invaders, could be seen in silhouette; or where, sometimes, a single Indian, galloping at full speed in the distance, became no more than a speck crawling along the rim of the prairie.

. . . And wherever the steel went, the settlers followed with their tents and their tools, their cattle and their kittens, their furniture and their fences.

PIERRE BURTON, FROM THE LAST SPIKE, PP. 109 AND 220

. . . As we slowly trudged through each day, each and every one of us spent some time day-dreaming. Our minds wandered into the future and the dreams helped us to overcome the frustrations of dirt, wind, short tempers and jumpy horses. Those who came more prepared than others shared their knowledge and belongings. Those who came ill-equipped coped as a result of that sharing.

. . . We have been humbled by the landscape and weather, yet we are proud of what we have accomplished. Our accomplishment is great, but it is put into perspective when we look across the never-ending prairie skyline.

NANCY RUSSELL, LETTER FROM 1982 WAGON TREK, JULY 1

The only word to describe the landscape here is flat. We decided to camp in a field near a slough about 20 miles north of Moose Jaw at 5:00. There wasn't a cloud in the sky for the entire day. Two colors dominate this country—blue sky and green landscape. That green belongs to grass, for there are very few trees. Throughout the day I spotted small bluffs of trees in the distance and counted the hours, yes hours, until we were close. The land and sky go on forever. It's quite overwhelming but at the same time difficult to appreciate because of the heat.

NANCY RUSSELL, LETTER FROM 1982 WAGON TREK, JUNE 21

Henning is sick and tired but that is no more than could be expected. Ibeth is the one who stood the whole trip the best all along. Well when we came to the last station and we were all put out into a raging blizzard we all cried, but then Papa was there.

It is so bare and strange on this wild prairie, in a way it reminds one of the ocean. . . . Our only room is twelve by sixteen feet in size so that is all the room we have to roam about in. There is a table and a bench nailed up along the wall. Two beds are arranged one above the other in one corner and I have hung curtains up around them which makes them look like a four poster. We are pioneers and as such we must be prepared to live.

JULIE FEILBURG, LETTER HOME TO DENMARK, MAY 28, 1911

I don't believe it is normal even here to have a snowstorm in May but it does happen. Last year they say they got a good layer of snow in mid June and had it not been for that they would not have had a crop for that was the last moisture they got till harvest time. . . .

We have had a snowstorm, a heatwave, high winds, rain, terrible sand storm, hail, thunder and lightning and a sudden cyclone that made the trap door on the cellar hole flap up and down. We seldom have two days alike so if that is the world's healthiest climate, as they say it is, then it certainly is not the most pleasant.

JULIE FEILBURG, LETTER HOME TO DENMARK, JULY 12, 1911

The house still stood upon the lonely hill
as I remembered it from long ago.
But now like some forlorn, unwanted waif,
it drooped dejected, and irresolute
before the buffeting of prairie winds.
The hollow windows stared like sightless eyes
across the years of pestilence and drought. . . .

The house is dark, and faceless shadows sway
in rooms where only memories remain.
No welcome voice cries from the open door,
but from the haunting years of yesterday
a plaintive piper's melancholy call;
nostalgic notes of unalloyed lament
that linger in the lonely heart of man
like fragrance of a half-remembered spring.

DOUGLAS BANHAM, FROM "THE OLD HOMESTEAD"

. . . The wind strains colors,

weaving them into the lilt

of a thousand flutes.

Flamboyant prairie,

heavy with grain,

bows and dances

through the endless summer.

C. M. BUCKAWAY, FROM "THE WIND FLUTES"

The sky tonight

Is filled with sparks,

That shatter through the inky blue,

And rust red-hot amidst the stars,

To vanish there—in smoky shroud . . .

R. J. HODGSON, FROM "THUNDERSTORM AT NIGHT"

This I remember—

The thunder and the hushed, the terrified waiting—

Then an opalescent curtain of rain

Draped from the roughened eaves . . .

NINA BERG, FROM "SASKATCHEWAN"

It was a cloudy, cold night with a strong wind blowing and, as he came into the open air, his nostrils contracted to the acrid smell of burning grass and wild weeds; from far away came the dreaded crackling of the prairie fire.

He hurried to the summit of the knoll and, a mile or more to the eastward, he saw the long line of flame, feeding on the thick old bottom of the buffalo grass, rushing onward on the wings of the gale. . . .

The flames were very close and the spectacle a fearsome one. The main fire was burning the grass down to the roots. The wind gusts were throwing the tongues of flame far ahead, and as they caught in the grass tops, they made a deep line of fire, shooting high in the air.

Z. M. HAMILTON, FROM THESE ARE THE PRAIRIES, P. 257

The crackling was tremendous, the heat overpowering and the clouds of smoke made respiration difficult. The lurid light threw everything into clear relief; the frightened horses plunged; the children screamed, and everyone stood by with wet grain sacks ready to beat out any fire in dangerous proximity to the building. Then almost in a moment it was past. It split at the ploughed guards and rushed off on each side, roaring down the wind. . . .

"Well," said Hicks, drawing a grimy hand across a blackened brow, "we have a lot to be thankful for. Nobody hurt and we have saved the live stock and gear. . . ."

Reid was reputed rather pious, and there were tears of real emotion making tracks on his smoke-blackened cheeks when he said: "God has been good to us once more."

"Aye!" said Hicks. "He has at that. I guess He knew how damned little we had."

Z. M. HAMILTON, FROM THESE ARE THE PRAIRIES, PP. 258-59

. . . We would stand shivering under
stars that hung low on invisible threads
    and listen as the distant train whistle
stirred and tugged at us with its haunting sound.

The Pool map hung on the kitchen wall,
a maze of railway lines and tiny towns
    strung together like beads
waiting for the horse-drawn wagons.
    Children grew up, the old ended their days
dreaming of the railway's vanishing point,
irresistibly drawn by the heady throb
    of the engine's thunder.

Then came expanding farms, big diesel trains and trucks
    and rail abandonment.
Small towns set adrift from the mainstream of travel;
the young lured to distant places.
Grass grows between the ties
    while down the track's perspective
winds whistle a dirge to yet another prairie town
    pushed slowly to its death.

THELMA HOFSTRAND FOSTER, FROM "PRAIRIE RAIL ABANDONMENT"

They gather each morning
at the back of the old store
where a window
outlines grass-fringed slopes
and patchwork strips.

Joe Blostenik has never missed
Tuesday's cattle auctions or a rodeo
since he stepped out of his stirrups
eight years ago.

And Hank whose asthma
drove him early
to his house in town
wheezes each slow step
to the end of the street.

They listen to the tap
of old Bill's cane
the tap as repetitious
as his tales of the thirties
that ride cigarette smoke
across the room.

These men who meet
stir lost dreams inside their cups
and are never more than a window
or one last story
away from the land.

DORIS BIRCHAM, "COFFEE ROW"

Prairie trails:

lesions upon a land

that mends with wind and dust

scars etched by weighted wagons

ART SHEPHERD

18

. . .

I've watched you shovel wheat,

      heavy, golden

spilling like liquid

      over the sides of the shovel,

the sweat trickling off your forehead,

      making trails

through the dust-cover

      on your cheeks. . . .

DORIS BIRCHAM, FROM "FATHER"

There ain't a hell of a lot of lookin' down,
livin' on the prairie. Every time you lower your eyes
to the ground, they're drawn to an ever-expanding view
that flattens to a horizon of land and sky. Kinda
causes you to look ahead—even more, to *over*head.
The prairie is simply a floor for a dome of sky,
a pasture for the wind to run across. Nope!
If you lean to lookin' down on things,
the prairie ain't the place to be.

ART SHEPHERD

The sleeping soil
is pulled from its lie
by a roguish wind
becomes a silver dust
lining for the horizon eye
of the prairie

while a tapestry of fire
is woven
   from the blood
of sun and dusk . . .

LINDA CHRISTIE, FROM "THE SAVAGE SUNSET"

. . .
a plum tree by the doorstep
leans towards the kitchen window
while sunlight across the table
warms a painting on the wall

*

what then do we leave
behind us in this place

spring water on the hillside
a few scarred trails
fingerprints in stone
a washboard   broken pottery
a tree groping for the clouds
and the forever wind that holds
the shapes of all our hands

DORIS BIRCHAM, FROM "SHAPES OF OUR HANDS"

The wind pushed the day toward the flat horizon
    Minutes rolled to hours with thistles and sage.
Dust devils tugged deep rooted dreams
    Throwing them to the wind in swirling rage. . . .

We tasted the day between our teeth.
    The prairie was on the move, running fast.
It screamed at windows decaying on the sills.
    A cardboard box from somewhere gave up and flew past. . . .

The brown day slid noisily into black night.
    The bold wind died. The stars came out with light
Falling a message. New hope was sprinkled.
    The morning dawned grey and cloudy. It rained before night.

DAVID KAISER, FROM "THREE DAYS OF WIND"

In late March these cute little rascals came up out of their holes for their spring romp, and every kid became a gopher hunter, not for fun alone, but for profit. . . .

Because of the destructive nature of the beast (each gopher eats about a dollar's worth of wheat a year, and so, on a section of land this amounts to a combined loss of more than three thousand dollars), municipalities usually pay from one to three cents for the destruction of a gopher, proof being possession of the tail. In 1933 the price of gopher tails like that of wheat was rock-bottom low. One cent. . . .

Sometimes a shrewd hunter would amputate the tail and let the gopher go, in the hope that he might grow another. As far as I know, this never worked. . . .

So, as the children presented me with these shaggy little wisps of hair, bone and blood, I shoved them into a bottom drawer of the desk against the day when I'd be able to take them to town.

MAX BRAITHWAITE, FROM WHY SHOOT THE TEACHER, PP. 129-31

Too hot—we complain
As we hurry from one
Air-conditioned building
To another.

We forget
Others who slaved
On open prairies—
Relentless sun
Upon bent backs,
Carving our future
Out of prairie grass.

MARY HARELKIN, "HEAT WAVE"

I saw the homestead just once after we left it to go back into town in the bitter fall of 1919. In the spring of 1920 we came past it on our way to Montana and camped in the shack for one night. . . . Our visit was not meant to change anything, or restore for an instant the hope we had given up. We merely passed through, picked up a few objects that we wanted, touched things with our hands in a reminding way, stood looking from the doorway down across the coulee. . . . We told ourselves that some day we would be back. We memorized the landmarks of five years.

WALLACE STEGNER, FROM <u>WOLF WILLOW</u>, PP. 282-83

But we knew, we all knew, that we wouldn't be back any more than the families of our acquaintance who had already left; and I imagine we obscurely felt that more than our personal hope had died in the shack that stayed in sight all the time we were bumping down along the field to the border. With nothing in sight to stop anything, along a border so unwatched that it might have been unmapped, something really had stopped there; a crawl of human hope had stopped. . . .

. . . My mother drew in her breath and blew it out again with a little laugh, and said the words that showed us how such a departure should be taken. "Well," she said, "better luck next time!"

WALLACE STEGNER, FROM WOLF WILLOW, P. 283

The city

ends
abruptly

The amputated
streets

leave me the odd
feeling

more was there
But all I see

is the stretching
cool black sea

of the prairie
and now and then

that beckoning
light

LEONA FUM

NATIVE TREASURES

There are some who gave up and abandoned the prairie, but there are others who draw their strength from the land. For them, it provides a sense of freedom, space to move, and a place to grow, feeding body and soul alike, imposing no limits. But it also offers little place to hide. No matter where you are, you stand exposed to the elements, vulnerable to the heavens.

It is only the hills that afford protection, and it is in the hills where we find an abundance of native treasures—a legacy of Indian artifacts and a wealth of flora and fauna. If you step slowly and observe, the land will reveal its treasures. Arrowheads, medicine wheels, and teepee rings take you back to an age forgotten. Brown-eyed susans, white-tailed deer, and blue-blue skies transport you to another world where Nature displays her finest jewels. Sometimes when I photograph these sacred places, I become spellbound, unable to continue. A silent voice whispers, "Not here, not now, just listen."

Another sanctuary brimming with treasure is the river. Because of the extensive flatness of the land, even the larger rivers tend to meander across the Great Plains. One giant among them is the Saskatchewan. Like a huge unruly shoelace, it threads its way through the many patches of colour that make up the fabric of the land, tying the Canadian Rockies to the foothills, the badlands, the grasslands, the sandhills, and the parklands, and finally weaving its way through the muskeg flats of the Precambrian Shield before joining Hudson Bay and the Arctic Ocean. As one of the great river systems of this continent, it knows intimately the beauty of the prairie, its banks as sacred to the present-day artist as they were to yesterday's Cree and Ojibway hunters.

The foundation from which all else springs, perhaps our greatest native treasure is the soil, generating the nutrients for an abundance of crops upon which nations across the world depend.

Here, then, are our "Native Treasures."

I've come to dream, and think of quiet . . .

I only long for the places

I belong for on this earth

Like the Sanctuary Plains

Where the quiet still remains

On the belly of the land . . .

GRAEME CARD, FROM "THE HYMN OF WAKANTANKA"

In summertime I walk up here   aware
another walked here long ago
the rocks that formed her teepee ring
lie still half-buried in the sod

now mine   this was her lookout point
I see the valley through her ancient eyes
I heard the sounds she heard   larks   hawks
and crickets   and the silky rhythm
of moccasins on sun-dried grass

this is a holy place
her sanctuary   mine
her chant is in my bloodstream
this song is a duet

LOUISE KOZROSKI, "SPIRIT LINK"

I am the old one.
I stand with my head held high
and branches spread toward the sky.
The youngers, small, stand below me,
seeds of me, my children.
Once when I was young
I stood with my brothers
but now they lie dead.
And here I stand—the old one. . . .

HEIDI MILLER, FROM "I AM THE OLD ONE"

This is the record of the barren years, . . .
        . . . But something yet remains,
Erect, in grim relief, that does not yield,
Like a gaunt rock worn by the winds and sands,
The will invincible that still disdains
Defeat, and in the heart of desolation stands
Immovable, and will not quit the field.

F. TALBOT SMITH, FROM "DROUGHT"

My lips touch on the water;
it moves with sensuous flow.
My hands I place on out-thrust rock—
it warms with phosphorescent glow.
I twine my arms with limb of tree
and feel life's tremble.
                    I am Cree.

The moon I worship
and call each star by name.
With grass and breeze I play
a laughing, running game.
Great Manitou gives with grace
each thing a spirit and a face.
                    I am Cree.

LEONORA HAYDEN MCDOWELL, "I AM CREE"

each year our machines
rearrange the relics
rain lashes the hillside
     again   again
and one day a scarred stone washes up clean
and pulls my hand toward it

through your tepee flap poplar smoke rises
iskwew   woman
I am a strange vision in your dreams
I see the muscles in your brown arms
as you ply the pelts

                         my fingers
curl around the curve
thumb against the edge
as if it were mine . . .

rivulets trace snake tracks across the hill
always different
always the same
the scraper is real

MARILYN CAY, FROM "TWO WOMEN ON THE HILL"

You know, the Indians are a strange people. They think the rocks have life. And when they go out onto the prairie and they shoot a deer, or a rabbit or a bird in the sky, they thank that animal. Would we go to an abattoir? They never got into real estate because they thought no one could own the land. You could not own the land! It belonged to Wankan Tanka, the Mysterious Force, the Great Spirit. Gitchi Manitou. The Voice of Silence. And the circle of it, where the circle of the tipis were, swept around the People and spread itself out flat, or hilly, with trees or without trees. The Great Prairie.

GRAEME CARD, FROM IN THE BLUE NIGHT SOUP I CAN HEAR THE NIGHT HAWK WHISTLE, P. 4

. . . Once I walked beside you through deep coulees,

dodging badger holes and gopher mounds.

We watched white-tails edge along a clearing

saw antlered heads turn, white flags flash

then blur towards the distance. . . .

DORIS BIRCHAM, FROM "FATHER"

Dawn grey curtains part,

Reed music sounds as the dancer appears.

Orange fringes her yellow dress,

Green binds her hair

But her shoes are crimson. . . .

VESTA PICKEL, FROM "AUTUMN BALLET"

Once the circle of the earth was the prairie, the edges lit with sky. And the tipi was a circle in the circle. Now the circle of the earth has touched the limits of the air and melts into space, and mankind stand on the planets that stand above the circle. And the People are looking at the circle of the universe and are saying, "This is my place and it is the tipi of Wakan Tanka, the Voice of Silence." And, as the mystery deepens, so the People get strong again and are given survival back into their hands.

GRAEME CARD, FROM IN THE BLUE NIGHT SOUP I CAN HEAR THE NIGHT HAWK WHISTLE, P. 30

It wouldn't be so bad, Brian thought, if a person knew, or even knew what it was that he wanted to know. . . . A thing couldn't come closer through a crazy man gone crazy from the prairie. Who cared about anybody living in a piano box on the bald-headed prairie?

And yet for breathless moments he had been alive as he had never been before, passionate for the thing that slipped through the grasp of his understanding and eluded him. If only he could throw his cap over it; if it were something that a person could trap. If he could lie outstretched on the prairie while he lifted one edge of his cap and peeked under to see. That was all he wanted—one look. More than anything!

W. O. MITCHELL, FROM WHO HAS SEEN THE WIND, PP. 198-99

The sun spilled up its slow light from below the eastern horizon, draining the darkness from the autumn sky. No shadow formed yet round the still, silent figure standing alone on the prairie, a girl of twelve, watching and waiting. An immense silence heeded itself through and around her. The deep earth upheld her feet, its resonance thrumming in stately measures like a prelude to magnificence.

A fingertip of light touched the meeting-point of earth and sky. It drew a small, bright line. Above it a cloud swelled into view, blue-black against the paling sky, an immense triangle with its point on the horizon. From there it spread toward her, reaching wide in a broadening canopy which filled nearly the whole sky, making vaster the vastness, widening the very width.

She could not take it in, yet she had to, it was her duty. Greatly she tried, stretching her vision, pressing open her mind, reaching as mightily as reached the cloud until she flowed into it and her body was a mere point of stillness, scarcely breathing, yet the centre of it all.

In that stillness she heard the far music, the sound of the sun, ascending in fire. The radiance burst into her face. She closed her eyes and became a sheet of flame.

PATRICIA JOUDRY, FROM THE SELENA TREE, PP. 166-67

He wanted to get down and run across the drying prairie, to roll in the matted, dun-coloured grass, to search with his fingers in it for the first sprouts of green. He wanted that morning back weeks ago when he had stumbled into the house, out of breath, forgetting even to pull off his boots.

"The coulees are running, Ma! The coulees are running!" he had shouted, and even his silent mother had put down her broom and followed him outside into the winter brilliance; . . . For months the sun had hung cool and white or the palest cream just above the horizon; involuntarily now they lifted their faces to its new warmth.

SHARON BUTALA, FROM THE GATES OF THE SUN, PP. 7-8

*I do set my bow in the cloud, and it shall
be for a token of a covenant
between me and the earth.*   Genesis 9:13

> Bracelet of beauty
> emeralds hung high
> token of love
> woven of teardrops
> joy from earth's pain
> eternal promise, ever the same.

EUNICEMARY MOORE

Brown-eyed susans
Breathed upon by God
Explode into birds
Singing life.

Yellow-brown
Not tied down
They fly their colours
Dropping their songs
Like nectar on the ground.

DAVID KAISER, "MIRACLE"

where grass clings to earth
where moss phlox hides beneath the grass
and wind half dries the buds
before they bloom
where badgers belly the earth
and churn the yellow grass

we dance

THELMA POIRIER, "PRAIRIE HENS"

46

bergamot is a punk flower
its head is a cluster of lavender spikes
bobbing in August,
a plot of dancers in the meadow
all show, no scent
bees sting their brain
set them dancing
to a hot sun
it is the last day of summer
a celebration of bergamot

THELMA POIRIER, "BERGAMOT"

I stood on the prairie
Every morning till dark
One day
For six weeks,
Working on my dream.
For that entire time
The wind
Tried to blow me down.
And it succeeded.

ERIC NYGREN, "DREAMS"

The river flows,
tracing alluvial dawns,
in even tempo,
ageless and unworrying
and silent as the sky. . . .

I can remember
when my bare feet,
washed by your waters,
left countless little footprints
in the moist clay.
Here, through innumerous days,
the burning summers
and carefree idling,
blended into dreams . . .

WILLIAM CONKLIN, FROM "SASKATCHEWAN RIVER"

In meadowlark morning,
the prairie hatches the sun.
It wears anklets of daisies
and patiently waits for
the sapphire of bluebells,
and the crimson of wild roses.
In secret places, violets grow
irridescent beneath the sky.

C. M. BUCKAWAY, "THE PRAIRIE IS ALSO A GARDEN"

My mother, she's the wind
She's a breathing, blowing, flying
Striving blue

My father is the silence of the earth
He's a sleeping, giving
Quiet being

And he's brown
To her blue
They love each other

LEONA FLIM, "LANDSCAPE"

Autumn stretches out
its talisman of days
all dressed in golden robes.
Dawn splits the long grass
of meadows, unties the sun.
The heat-pulled wind
throbs like fire on this land.

Weeds cluster in shards
scratching and creaking,
copper-toned and old.
Trash fires blur the air—
leaves paint quiet footprints
on a golden land.

Wild geese fleck the skies
with black embroidery—
stitched forever
in their southern flight.

On the sides of the hills
crimson flow of cranberries
glows in riotous tangles.
Prairie, shot with autumn,
bears its gifts, its smiles,
to the swift tide of winter.

C. M. BUCKAWAY, "THE GOLDEN TALISMAN"

You cannot pack
  a cricket
  or a tumbleweed;
  nor sand-silt
  on a windowsill;
  high bright skies
  and hot dry winds;
  low dark clouds
  and hailstones;
  a prickly rose;
  nodding brown-eyed susans;

steel ribbons
and grey slab fences;
fiery sunsets;
cool nights;
yellow fields
with room galore!
These are native treasure,
Not trinkets for a tourist's pleasure.

PHYLLIS SHERRING, "HOMECOMING"

Wheatfields shimmer 'neath the everchanging sun.
Boxcars, cavernous for the golden flow
Snake across the stubble
And through the craggy cliffs.

Hungry ships are waiting,
Great vessels for the bounty of the Prairies,
Breadbasket to the tables of the world.

GRACE MILNE, "BREADBASKET"

DAYDREAMS

A daydream is an altered state of consciousness. For me there are two kinds of daydreams—reflections and reveries. The former involves thought and memory, putting things together for yourself, working out an answer to a problem, or plotting new strategies to cope with life's complexities. Reverie is quite a different process; it is a blanking of the mind, a getting in touch with the higher self through silent meditation. By surrendering ego, one can melt into the landscape, become a living, breathing part of it.

Both the magnitude of the prairie skies and the omnipresence of the land draw us easily into daydreams, and perhaps the horizon line can be seen as a symbolic division between the two types. Casting our eyes downward to the land, the animals, plants, and flowers give us cause to ponder, encouraging us to reflect on process, explore mechanics, and ask the often unanswerable why. I have learned a great deal from sharing my yard with several dozen gophers, an entire community of wildlife visible from my doorstep. They eat, chase, tussle, keep watch, chatter, sun themselves, squeak warnings, and forage. I observe their autumn activities that indicate their sure knowledge of the approaching winter, and their carefully timed escapes from marauding magpies.

Raising your eyes to the sky, however, short-circuits those thought patterns; you stop thinking and start feeling. If you look to the land for assurance, it is to the sky that you turn for promise. A prairie sky is an archway to the universe, its nightly theatre a window to the galaxies, and our most tangible link to the elusive heavens. In the crisp clean air of a frosty winter morning we can almost feel their closeness. Nothing is more pure and fine.

Photography has taught me the importance of being out there, regardless of inclement conditions. Prairie dreaming, likewise, is not an armchair activity; its only prerequisite, in fact, is being there. It requires you, an active participant, to take a walk, climb a hill, or find a viewpoint. Then, through the silence of a winter night or the brilliance of an August dawn, your inner voice will speak.

Dreaming is a timeless activity. This chapter opens with a radiant dawn and moves through a day of reflections and reveries. And then, like country folk, we will sit on the porch and quietly watch the dust of another day's labour slowly settle into darkness, listen to the sound of the crickets, and experience the bliss of perfect stillness. Though this land of earth and sky stretches far beyond our grasp, perhaps in a dream it still is knowable.

I saw the wind run down the hill,
I heard the sun come up with song.
Let jeer who must, and scoff who will,
I saw the wind run down the hill.
I chatted with a daffodil
The grassy silences among;
I saw the wind run down the hill,
I heard the sun come up with song.

EDNA C. HANSON, "SUNRISE"

I am pierced through
  by prairie light
chained by meadowlarks
  with gold and silver loops
hobnailed to the sod
  by sturdy steel-grey crocus
and bound to be
      to be free
in this singing   limitless   space

LOUISE KOZROSKI, "GULLIVER IN SPRINGLAND"

. . . birches
reach arthritic fingers
towards a dappled sky
in an offering of
weathered palms

Stylized branches
splintering the prairie
to catch at the dawn
and draw down morning

JESSICA SLIGHTS, FROM "ABOUT SASKATCHEWAN . . ."

My endless daily duties press
Against my will, and rile
My patience till I long to leave
Reality a while.
In my dream world, unspanned by man,
I roam among the trees—
Relaxed . . . sequestered . . . where I do
Exactly as I please . . .

ALICE DEROO, FROM "I REST AWHILE"

Divided
by a fence line
two ranchers disagreed
where
barbed wire should be stretched
and over the years their cattle
strayed to the wrong side.
A gate rubbed open, a broken wire
left holes like unhealed wounds.

There may have been
fewer silences and sharp words
had they known
their headstones would be separated
not by barbed strands
but by one thin band
of prairie.

DORIS BIRCHAM, "NEIGHBORS"

My window frames a hill,
a three-dimensional photograph
that changes with each season.

Its grass-fringed cover, greened in spring
turns crisp under August sun
when rosebrush blends russet shades.
Later, winter shadows soften edges,
purple the snowdrifts piled in draws. . . .

DORIS BIRCHAM, FROM "MY HILL"

The unclaimed silence, save for lone loon's cry,
invites both earth and man to seek togetherness.
Lean ribbed giants dominate a leafy world;
gritty toes, soil proof to sun and rain, anchor roots
to straining fibers of wilderness terrain. . . .

JOAN A. HAMILTON, FROM "WHERE PALE LIGHT BREAKS"

The wind sighs through me, as though
I were an opening in the tangible air,
a space in space . . .
it threads its way through me,
ties me to the horizons . . .

Through me are borne
wild rose and willow song,
parachuting seeds
and wings.

LOUISE KOZROSKI, "EYE OF THE NEEDLE"

sometimes i wish for winter
to last right through june
i want to squeeze the western clouds
for one more fall of snow

but then spring comes rushing in
and i have to think again

winter holds more safety
preserving every step in ice
giving frozen excuses for being
just the same as in the past

while spring rivers run down my street
playing at the edges of my old

winter's death and cold appeal
for i can shrug so tightly down
cold shouldering life and love
muffling every new birth sound

yet spring dives down with robins
singing new songs to the day

icy roads keep me grounded
and making sound and pious judgments
daring not to rush so much
bundled in my comforter

spring comes blushing with crocuses
kicking skyward in footprints of colour

stepping gingerly winter slows
my fearful steps so i dare not walk
in bold new paths or even stop much
lest i break routine

then spring bubbles into puddles
begging me to jump in like a kid again . . .

DAVID KAISER, FROM "SPRING, I'VE HAD SOME SECOND THOUGHTS"

Desolate? Forbidding? There was never a country that in its good moments was more beautiful. Even in drouth or dust storm or blizzard it is the reverse of monotonous, once you have submitted to it with all the senses. You don't get out of the wind, but learn to lean and squint against it. You don't escape sky and sun, but wear them in your eyeballs and on your back. You become acutely aware of yourself. The world is very large, the sky even larger, and you are very small.

WALLACE STEGNER, FROM WOLF WILLOW, P. 8

This warm grey
June day
is shot with colour like an eastern shawl:
deep wild-rose pink and
dandelion gold,
foxglove magenta,
clover creamy-white . . .
and all among the drowsy flower-filled fields
dart swallows with the sunset on their breasts,
while high in that dark fir tree like a spire
a hummingbird reveals his flash of fire.

MARY COLEMAN, "DESIGN ON A GREY BACKGROUND"

. . . Does this mechanical thirst-quencher
ever feel the urge to shift its
fearless gaze during its timed rotation,
or perhaps the wild impulse to
break loose and pantomime a
clumsy rain dance, knowing full well
God has forgotten about southern Alberta?

KATHLEEN SMITH, FROM "IRRIGATION"

old cow chewing cud . . .
we stare at each other
I smile
she chews
we've known each other
a long time

the noise of the yard is far away
I lean back and sigh
the rest of the herd
(hers and mine)
are busy
she switches flies
I explore her dark eyes
our world is time and space
away
from anybody else's race

MARILYN CAY, FROM "A WORLD UNSEEN"

the sun strains on the coldest day
rising late
grumpily she takes
her vicious dogs
and walks the sky, their path
barely arches over trees

the dogs run ahead at noon
at five o'clock she bobs
like a round red balloon
on the horizon
then slips suddenly and is gone
leaving us with our fears

MARILYN CAY, "THE SUN AND HER DOGS"

. . . it is evening on the prairies,
I can identify the sounds.
I hear my neighbour, John Dahl, hammering nails
      into his granary,
And my other neighbour, the meadowlark, calling and
      answering from his fence-post.

Then comes the silence—
Silence so solid I can hold it in my hand.
So pure I can drink it like springwater.
I know I am at home.

LILA CARROLL, FROM "PRAIRIE SILENCE"

. . . how fine being dirty
on a last harvest eve,
the strong smell of diesel spilling over my hands.
It drags me back to the world.

Mystery is where it's coming from,
Mystery is where it's going;
and the coyotes feel it
yodelling late in their dens,

and the geese in the sky,
the trout in the slough,
all leaping and flapping
from the depth
of their rites,
enacting the soundless, brilliant laughter.
Or like me, just filling
an old diesel drum,
careless with wonder
in the midst of it all.

R. CLARK, FROM "FILTH AND THE HOLY"

How long can a dream wait
Ere the bloom of it goes?
Ere the glow of it glimmer and die
Like the last autumn rose . . .
How long can a dream live?
Through the laughter and song,
Through the hatred and sorrow and tears
A dream can live long . . .
How long will a dream wait?
From the seed to the sheaves,
Till hopes fall away one by one
Like the last autumn leaves.

EDNA C. HANSON, "DREAMS"

. . . All nature gives birth in springtime;
breaking thin winter's hold
on stones embedded for centuries.
A giant jig-saw rise
and flow of life,
odor of newness—
a journey upwards
with the winged ones
in rainless skies. . . .

C. M. BUCKAWAY, FROM "CROCUSES IN THE SNOW"

. . . the air is resin tanged

a coyote howls—bringing back

memories of a vanished time

there is a glow on the black water

and suddenly I feel the tears of autumn.

BERT WILSON, FROM "SASKATCHEWAN RIVER"

Cicadas burr, the August haze
makes clover, goldenrod, and hay
sweeter, and the cicadas faint
until they only bring in stillness:
these are the last of the long days.

Summer insists, asserts: the heat
keeps coming; but the haze is new,
the stillness different, a sweet haunting:
winds and sparks of equinox:
these are the last of the long days.

Grain trickles to the bins; they fill;
haze thickens; the cicadas hum:
these are the best of the long days:
if cakes get baked or high thoughts come
all's well, all's well if nothing comes.

ROBERT BEUM, "INTERIM"

Priest
Blooded altar
Field mouse!
Half-ton chanter—
                    Hawk
                  Hangs
                      High
Egyptian Ra
        Saskatchewan sky!

STAN CHOPIK

She stopped at last and braced her feet and threw her arms to the east and west, then turned her face up, smiling, and opened like a flower to the sun. The sky of bright polished blue was filled with singing and the music poured into her like liquid from a jug, filling her all the way to her toes and the ends of her fingers, so that she sang too, without uttering a sound. . . . Far out where the grain was planted a sheet of gold lay spread upon the land. She turned the other way and saw that the golden sheet had wrapped itself around the world and come back and joined itself. . . .

She threw herself out full length on her back and shut her eyes. Small golden flowers sifted onto her eyelids. She listened and heard the singing of the deep earth. It was humming and thrumming in tune with the air and she was in tune with it all.

PATRICIA JOUDRY, FROM THE SELENA TREE, PP. 129-30

there's something rather strange and still
about a warm winter afternoon
when the sun has dipped until
there is only a subtle peach haze on the
clouds
and a silver sparkle on the trees
      the snow is soft
with endless rills and rolls
and tracks
birds hush
for a change, and listen

animals smile with their gentle eyes
        and people
           people
look and look
and take off their mitts
and adjust their hats
and breathe deeply
trying to grasp it
I wonder if warm winter afternoons
mean this much everywhere
or just here

MARILYN CAY, "STRANGE AND STILL"

so pretty
you could lick up
blueberry sky
chicken gravy stubble
ice cream snow
to hell with the summer of 36
the autumn of 14
and the winter of 74
if a face were to appear
out of all the
clairol soft sexy trees
it would be the face of an angel . . .

DON KERR, FROM "WATERCOLOURS OF THE PRAIRIE"

. . . Withered limbs of aging, sap-drained trees tremble,
creak from sudden pressure-squeeze—
bold thrust of whim-filled wind.
Infant shadows creep to space and span
the dictates of a Northern prairie night.
The moon appears, an arc, rich and complete,
to curve the ordered growth of heart and mind.

JOAN A. HAMILTON, FROM "WHERE PALE LIGHT BREAKS"

TOO LONG WINTER

"Too Long Winter" is a synonym for hard work. Any season means toil and struggle if one depends on the elements for a livelihood. Ask any farmer about the hazards of spring planting, the threat of a late blizzard to newborn calves, or the devastation to the soil caused by a snowless winter. Summer, too, has its drawbacks—the threat of wind, tornados, hail, thunderstorms, grass fires, insect pests and other blights, and drought. One cannot help but wonder what keeps these souls on the farm year after year. But even though farming, at its best, offers mixed blessings, the payoff is in the sense of belonging, the closeness to the land, and the feeling that you're meant to be there.

If the prairie fosters a love-hate relationship, it also breeds a stock of hardy inhabitants. Summer demands patience and faith; harvest time calls for strength and endurance. But with winter comes the acid test, and the chilling winds of a December storm show no favourites between city and country dwellers. Everyone from Alsask to Zealandia knows the bite and peril of a winter blizzard, and downtown Winnipeg is as prone and exposed to the subarctic gales as is uptown Wymark.

In spite of modern-day improvements in transportation, farming practices, communications, education, and medicine, there is one factor that has not changed: dependence on the land. We still must rely on a good blanket of snow and steady June rain to assure our crops of a good germination. We depend on hot cloudless days in July to bring the grain to maturity, and we hold out the hope of bringing in the harvest before the grasshoppers or the hailstones perform their devastation. The need for Mother Earth and Father Sun to play their parts becomes critical. Without their cooperation, an entire season feels like too long winter. Because the prairie economy is highly dependent on the success of the farmer, we all feel the squeeze when the grain belt tightens. Conversely, the joys of a bumper year are shared by all.

This chapter begins with a glimpse of harvest in progress, then moves into winter, the longest of the prairie seasons, and a time when dreaming comes most easily. It is time to get prepared, to brace ourselves for hibernation; then, with visions of crocus blooms, we wait patiently for the heralding of spring.

The sun centers the sky
with its blue cover pinned
to the edge of the prairie.

Swaths a mile distant
lie in the field you planted
last spring each tractor round
numbering furrowed days.
And you said the meadowlarks
had never sung so clear before.

When rains came your wheat filled.
Your body wasted but your eyes
held the shape of autumn.

And now beside your casket
we stand
as three birds fly past
songs stilled beneath their wings
in the harvest afternoon.

DORIS BIRCHAM, "SEASONS"

We chose Saskatchewan prairie: a loneliness
to live for in an age that lived for noise—
a tree, a house, a face, something to bless,
the comfort of small comfort. Here were joys.

ROBERT BEUM, "LINES FOR A HEADSTONE"

Where earth and sky
Forever gaze
On one another—
Wide-eyed with wordless knowing
Of the other!
A place where vast
Horizons meet—
Rimming around
A ring complete!

Where the earth flows out
And skies cup over
Waving wheat or
Wind-blown clover;
Where meadowlarks
On flashing wing,
Roused from the long fawn grasses
Spring
In throaty joy:

And over sloughs and marshy fens
The lone loon
Cries,
And floods of crimson wash the western
Skies,
And roaming coyotes howl
Towards the moon,
And great winds walk
In the wide lands,
Where earth and sky
Forever gaze
On one another—
Wide-eyed with wordless knowing
Of the other!

VINA CHILTON. "PLAINS"

Facing flat earth
sliding south
we crouch
between the elevators
in spilled grain
waiting for wheels to
make flat copper badges

Kevin kneels in the cinders
ears on the track, he
hears the rumble
it whistles
from Kincaid
moves westward through Hazenmore
past us
never stopping
past Pontiex   westward

Cafe men warn
our pennies will trip the train
derail it
rupturing hoppercars
spilling flax   oats   wheat
through these dirt streets

Of course
we wait for this

We sure don't wait
for flattened pennies

RICK HILLIS, "ANEROID"

88

green manes of growing grain
waving like a sea
the rustle of the lanky heads
moving restlessly
in the evening when the sun slips
leaving red along the line
a farmer stands with hands on hips
sees his labor, feels his time

MARILYN CAY, "FARMER AT SUNSET"

The northern lights storm:

whitecaps tipped with phosphorescence

Breaking over stars.

ANDREA HOLTSLANDER

The world is a silver penny
impossibly large
and I am in the middle of it.
A penny reaching from rim to dull grey rim of sky
that curves above my head, a lustreless bowl.
There is nothing but the snow and I.
The snow in shadowed hummocks is its superscription,
but I cannot read the language nor make out the
                design.
I am alone in this white desolation.
Though I move it travels with me,
featureless,
and I still remain in the middle.

MARGOT OSBORN, "PRAIRIE IMPRESSIONS"

91

White spun cotton candy

Coats licorice trees—

Sticks to car windows—

Covers the earth

Sugar white against

Whipped-cream clouds.

It melts—fades away

With the first lick of

Morning sun that peeps

Through the clouds onto

The sugar-frosted earth.

MARY HARELKIN, "HOAR FROST"

the wind is a sigh
too long winter
your sunsets are painted
with soft strokes of
pink, peach, promising warmth but
tomorrow is always cold
always winter

I listen for sounds of water
trickling
rushing
far away dreams
childhood
distant as the horizon

MARILYN CAY, "TOO LONG WINTER"

fog covers her flanks in the morning
she lies, still dozing . . .

how peaceful she looks
as the sun quivers on the rim
the beams showing rosey-red
pastures, expansive fields
it pleases us to say
we own her

atop the balestack I watch her wake
    trying to feel detached
    trying not to feel the rush
    of energy as day breaks
    she waits for nothing
    she feeds on time
    my hours belong to her . . .

MARILYN CAY, FROM "THE FARM"

I got winter in my bones.
They is long and white,
So hard they snap like ice.
But inside-a them,
There run like a river,
A little froze—but not complete,
That there's the marrow meat.
That there's what winter's all about.

Long nights,
The wind bites at you like it gots teeth.
Needle teeth—freeze you white.
Your chin, your cheek, your ear.
So you stay inside the long winter.
In the day you can see the cold,
Like a million little icy-culls
Just hanging still in the air.
And the sun is so hard
It pract'ly punch you in the eyeballs.

Even with no wind the air
Take your breath away.
It go out like a fog,
And you feel a little colder
Each time you breathe.
And your footsteps they crunch, crunch,
Like you walking in parcel packing.
It white and cold and it go on forever.

That's winter.
What I gots in my bones.
Can't shake it.
It go too deep.
Why, in summer when I sweats—
I know, that only an icy-cull
Melting.

MARY HORNE

Often in Saskatchewan a man awakens on a winter night hearing a great wind, and his heart sinks at the prospect of more shut-in days, more cold, difficulty, discomfort, and danger. But one time in ten, . . . when he opens door and storm door against the grab and bluster of the wind, the air rushes in his face as warm as milk, all but smelling of orange blossoms, and he dances a caper on his cold floor and goes back to bed knowing that in the two or three days that the chinook blows it will gulp all the snow except the heaviest drifts and leave the prairie dry enough to sit down on. . . .

Several times every winter the harsh Saskatchewan weather is relieved by that beautiful mild wind that can raise the temperature in a half hour from zero to fifty above. It is the chinook that makes Saskatchewan bearable in winter, the chinook that clears the prairies periodically and allows cattle to feed.

WALLACE STEGNER, FROM WOLF WILLOW, P. 220

This is horizon land. The prairies meet
Heaven without pretense. The line is neat,
Scissored, uncluttered as geometry
Could chart it. That is all there is to see.
A slice of earth and a great sweep of sky,
You, homeward-yearning, say as much to me,
Wondering, with audible distaste, why I
Live in the barren, Godforsaken place.
Your words belie creation. It was He
Who opened these wide skies for a window-space,
Kept crystal clean, in need of no adorning
With mountain drape or forest curtain-lace.
Here, for a heartbeat, on an April morning
He throws the shutters back and shows His face.

LILA CARROLL, "THE WINDOW"

My friends
The sun, the wind, and rain,
Did talk to me.
Clothed only in themselves,
They pressed on me a clarity.
Fleeting and lovely
They gave themselves without remorse.
Their yeast, that thing last learned.
Their gift, the guilt of wanting free
To be
The sun, the wind, the rain,
And me.

ERIC NYGREN, "DANCE"

Weary of winter, a lean, hungry thing

I'm following hope to the edge of the spring,

panning the breezes for riches untold—

sifting through birdsong for meadowlark gold.

LOUISE KOZROSKI, "PROSPECTOR"

on a still day
white violence explodes atop
swirling darkness, building higher
                              higher
dances dangerously over
      fields   this
      way and that
        will it
         touch
          down
           or
            p
             a
              s
               s

SEASONS WILL COME

It is easy to imagine prairie dreams expressed overtly in the sky, its dramatic theatrical backdrop offering a reflection of the human drama on the earth below. With unabashed grandeur, the sky gods perform; they swirl and dart, leap and dive, tumble and crash in an orchestrated dance of the heavens. Watching, we sense our own connection with the elements, feeling an inner stillness in the calm of a windless June morning, or the fragile, fleeting nature of our own mortality in the brief but perfect warmth of Indian summer.

The prairie sky comes in one size only: extra large. From the top of my camper I can sometimes see two or three eternities away. And when I stand with camera and tripod at sunset, I can see my five-legged shadow taper to a distant point more than fifty times my height. By the time the sun touches the western rim, my shadow has grown beyond measure, a symbolic image that helps define the psyche of prairie people. Visitors brand us as open, friendly. Perhaps the openness

comes from feeling we have the space to grow, the friendliness from knowing there's room to share. No matter where we stand in this vast space, we are always at the centre of a circle on a plane whose radius seems infinite.

Prairie folk strive to be masters of their destiny. We have the courage to take risks and a sense that our actions count. As an agriculturally based economy, we often see the products of our labours, and even if the dream sometimes wanes, the conviction remains strong. Our stubbornness is one of our great strengths, and our will power the prelude to achievement.

Perhaps our greatest dream is to live in harmony with the land and to retain the riches of our native treasures, a goal reflected in the unadorned words of a ten-year-old child. Jason AuBichon, in his letter to *Prairie Dreams,* wrote: "As an Indian I respect the land and what is on it. . . . My ancestors lived here before me, keeping the land and building a future for me. . . . I hope I can be as good to the land as it has been to me."

A few parched men, those few to whom a stone
Can tell an epoch's maddened, tortured tale,
Have used their lives to dig and dredge in shale
Of caves and gorges for a talking bone,
A fossil jaw, a skull—a tooth alone . . .
All bits and pieces of a brightening grail
Whose rays one day will pierce Time's final veil
And dawn-age Adam shall at last be known. . . .

RUTH SEIDLER, FROM "HORIZONS"

. . . I stand quiet, warmed
by the simple strength
of birds and trees.

As you lead your horse
along the path I see you
bend into the wind
and reach out your hand
to hold the feather.

DORIS BIRCHAM, FROM "GREY DAYS"

. . . I cannot sleep for the brown owls talking.
What do they say—
Asking a question—answering—
Softly and sadly in the dark?
Fly away, brown owls;
I do not wish to hear your voices
Nor feel your dream wings
Brush my frightened face.
The owls are quiet now.
Perhaps tomorrow afternoon
My grandmother will come—
Then sitting on the floor
             with feet stretched out,
We'll eat wild hazelnuts and
                      red rose hips.

DOROTHY MORRISON, FROM ''BROWN OWLS TALKING''

Is it really important for a boy to learn the name of a wild animal, what it eats, where it lives, and how it rears its young while at the same time the boy never gets to live near the animal? Would it not be better to let nature be, and let the boy live with unspoiled affection for all creatures, instead of teaching him to boast of knowledge?

CHIEF DAN GEORGE, "LET NATURE BE" FROM <u>MY HEART SOARS</u>, P. 28

The wind of spring rolls up a cloud of dust
  When I go planting on my quarter plot,
  Although it's little gain I ever got
From all my planting of this prairie crust.
They say I have a yen—a sort of lust—
  For poverty's lean porridge in the pot,
  Else I would pull my stakes, as well I ought.
But I am planted here and stay I must.

Blackfoot and Cree with men of older race
  Are down below my feet; only today
  I found three arrowheads. Dead men are near;
Their hands reach up and hold me to this place
  That when I lie with them, someone may say
  "The prairie grass is somewhat taller here."

ELLA M. DAVIS, "THE CALL OF THE GROUND"

Canadians hear much about their natural resources such as oil, forests, and minerals. Valuable as these are, the stuff for lack of which the world is most likely to suffer is not uranium or nickel or gold or petroleum or wood pulp, but good food-producing soil. Farm soil is Canada's most priceless possession. And of the nation's arable land, nearly three-quarters is in the midwest, between the region of the Red River and the Rocky Mountains. Thus western farms must be seen as the greatest of Canadian assets, a great world asset and the backbone of Canadian agriculture. Seasons will come and seasons will go, but a thousand years hence, if it rains, Canada may be fairly sure of a good crop of bread wheat between the Red and the Rockies, and a sturdy breed of farmers to grumble about the price and get right out on the land again in the following spring.

GRANT MACEWAN, FROM BETWEEN THE RED AND THE ROCKIES, P. 296

the storm banks
strong words
written on a paper sky
waiting for exposure
by an orator
who adds sound
and emotion
in the thunder
of his voice

the audience waits
each throaty phrase
seeking fresh thought
enlightened ideals
sceptics say it came too late
some anticipate change
a few are awed enough
they vow to modify
their politics

little children
puddle around the edges
laughing within season
enjoying the celebration
more
before it drys up
and breaks into nothing
but promises

DAVID KAISER, "SUMMER STORM"

our boat
glides slowly on amber glass

   silver threads
poke the surface
trailing hooks
but log fish only stare

along the shore
trees are dark dribbles
into water

MARILYN CAY, "STILL LIFE OF AUTUMN AFTERNOON AT LAKE"

111

a large crowd
of canadians
from way up north
gathered
for a few days
before heading
south

they gabbed
and honked
at the circus stilt
walkers
who entertained them
in no particular formation

at a distance
white snowy purists
sat aloof
watching but afraid
to budge
or smudge

very soon
differences not withstanding
they'd all vacation
in warmer climes
waiting spring

DAVID KAISER, "WINTER MIGRATION"

Snow lines in summerfallow

man and nature penning dreams

co-authors of next year

LOUISE KOZROSKI, "CALLIGRAPHY"

horses turn bums to the wind

winter coats fluffed back

baring skin

they huddle with trees

heads down

tails between their knees

MARILYN CAY, "PICTURE OF THE NORTH WIND"

114

. . . Poplar-trees are bare:

    caught in the moan of the wind

    amber scent of snow.

C. M. BUCKAWAY

Old wind, brown wind, wind of the weary Lent,
Blow, wind! Rave, wind!
Roll up your legions of dust, old wind,
And scream to your heart's content.
I have built my home on the fields of earth.
It is mine by the right of the plough,
And nothing—you hear me, old maker of mirth!
And nothing can frighten me now.

Old wind, brown wind, wind you are long and late.
Blow, wind! Rave, wind!
Roll up your legions of dust, old wind.
The sowing and I can wait.
In the lonely gloam of my empty mill,
I have heard you, you mock and you jeer.
But some day, old wind, you'll have whistled your fill,
And I and my plough will be here!

FRED E. LAIGHT, "SONG OF THE PRAIRIE PLOUGHMAN"

As an Indian I respect the land and what is on it. I have lived on the prairies all my life, and will remain here till my death. . . . I don't understand the land; I just see it as it is: rolling hills, golden sun, and wildlife. The prairies to me hold a certain sense of beauty that maybe some people don't see. . . . My ancestors lived here before me, keeping the land and building a future for me. . . . I love where I am, and always will. . . . I hope I can be as good to the land as it has been to me.

JASON AUBICHON

The sun
Soft and spring, and warm,
Flows gently through the window
That not long ago
Let little light or warmth
Into this room.
Half iced from winter's cold,
It did then but shelter us,
And make our makeshift cave
A solitary place to be.
But now the sun does warm,
Is spring and soft,
So life will multiply again.

The ache of winter's cramp,
Once harboured in the wind, and mind,
And bundled, slowing clothes,
Becomes the ache of doing.

So with everything
We were, and are, and will.
To last. To live.
To keep.

ERIC NYGREN, "TO YIELD"

It is a land
forever
the colour of ripe wheat
    a land
golden
smelling of crisp-crusted
bread
even in white of winter
when roads are cold
skating rinks small Toyotas
disapprove of.

It is a land
forever green
   a land
growing lush grass
        tender new barley
        fields of clover
in me   always
though no rain has fallen
three summers
in the hopeful south.

It is a land
forever me
forever giving me
forever inside
my own sweet heart of prairie
where even the nights are full
of sounds grown
golden
where even the skies are full
of green and of wheaten
stars.

GERTRUDE STORY, "PRAIRIE"

120

The sun slowly eases
toward the horizon
its radiance bright and clear
in its last few hours.
The farmer pauses,
watches in wonder
the brilliant weave
stretched out around him
waving, beckoning, splendid.
The grain is tawny, gleaming;
the farmer is uneasy.
Is it Mother Nature
spreading out her golden tablecloths
for hail and wind to dine?

PATRICIA COULTER, "GOLDEN TABLECLOTHS"

. . . Autumn colours, and a ripeness

too long out of mind;

a relief to be here now,

this gold and rust in time. . . .

R. CLARK, "APPLES"

The sinking sun cast long shadows. Its rays reflected
from the fly-speckled windows of Sam's tumble-down shack,
turning it into a house of golden windows—just as memory,
when focused on the pages of the mind, turns a very simple
childhood event into a golden treasure.

BRIDGET BIEM

Here are no pillars heaved by giant's might
up to cloud's kiss; no broken rainbow by
tall waterfall; no tattered patch of sky
affording star or two, to shed scant light
on valley farm or noisy canyon's night.
Not here those reservoirs of ice piled high
on peaks; not here small turquoise lakes that eye
may never view, lip touch nor wind affright.

Here is the world's great
          threshing floor. Pumps hear
oil's gurgle underneath. Jets plow for miles
across domed azure fields. Our sky, the place
where rainbows trace size of earth's hemisphere.
Our rivers loath to leave, by wandering wiles,
form mirrors where deer come to sip cloud's lace.

ANGELENA CAMPBELL, "OUR PRAIRIE"

. . . Sometimes
        she'd think of leaving
        go work in town . . .

    But when she thinks
    of a lost youth
    or never-to-be-seen places
    a coyote will call
    a voice in her night
    so she walks down to the barn
    just to watch her horses run . . .

    It was good, she whispers,
    I'll never go.

    THERESE ECKEL, FROM "THE FORGOTTEN"